100 YEARS OF MORTALITY

by

EDWIN C. HUSTEAD, F.S.A.

Society of Actuaries
475 N. Martingale Road
Schaumburg, Illinois 60173

Copyright 1989, Society of Actuaries.

All rights reserved by the Society of Actuaries. Permission is granted to make brief excerpts for a published review. Permission is also granted to make limited numbers of copies of material in this book for personal, internal, classroom or other instructional use, on condition that the foregoing notice is used so as to give reasonable notice of the Society of Actuaries' copyright. This consent for free limited copying without prior consent of the Society of Actuaries does not extend to making copies for general distribution, for advertising or promotional purposes, for inclusion in new collective works, or for resale.

Expressions of Opinion

Expressions of opinion stated in this book are those of the author, and are not the opinion or the position of the Society of Actuaries. The Society of Actuaries assumes no responsibility for statements made or opinions expressed in this book.

ISBN   0-938959-12-3

CONTENTS

Preface v

Introduction vii

I. Mortality in the United States 1

    Trends in Rates of Mortality 2
    Mortality from Birth to Age 35 10
    Mortality from Age 35 to Age 70 14
    Mortality after Age 70 16
    Life Expectancy in the
      Twentieth Century 19

II. Mortality Tables used by Actuaries
    in the United States 23

    Types of Mortality Tables 24
    British Mortality Tables Used in
      the United States 30
    American Experience Table 31
    Insurance Tables 33
      Individual Insurance 34
      Group Insurance 39
    Annuity Tables 41
      Individual Annuities 41
      Group Annuities 46
    Other Tables 50
      Industrial Insurance 50
      Fraternal Organizations 51
    Comparison of Tables 52

III. The Future of Mortality 57

    Gompertz and Other Laws
       of Mortality 58
    Is There a Maximum Life Span? 63
    Improvement in Mortality 69
    Mortality in the Twenty-First
       Century 71

Notes 79

Index to Mortality and Related
    Tables 87

PREFACE

Since the Society of Actuaries predecessor organization, the Actuarial Society of America, was formed 100 years ago, an amazing amount of change has taken place in society that has directly or indirectly impacted mortality in North America. The aggregate impact of these changes has been identified and applied by actuaries in their analysis and pricing of life insurance and annuities.

Historical changes affecting mortality have included war, improvements in our sanitary and water supply systems, our increasing standard of living and the expansion of medical science. A significant positive trend has been the identification of major risk health factors and the education of the public in their effects on personal health. As knowledge further progresses and society acts on that knowledge, mortality levels should continue to improve. On the other hand, other factors may develop that would adversely affect mortality. These include new diseases or epidemics (e.g., Human Immunodeficiency Virus) and environmental changes brought about by the accumulation of the side effects of modern society.

In this monograph, Edwin C. Hustead has done an admirable job of surveying and discussing the major mortality trends of the last 100 years and the reactions of actuaries to these trends. The development of appropriate mortality tables has led to the establishment and maintenance of sound bases for the products and the entire financial condition of the life insurance and employee benefits industries. Actuaries will continue to react to and anticipate trends in mortality, as well as other demographic and economic factors, in their expanding role in the financial services, employee benefit and health care industries.

Sam Gutterman, F.S.A.
Chairperson, Committee on Experience Studies,
Society of Actuaries

INTRODUCTION

This monograph was initiated as a result of discussions at the Committee on Experience Studies of the Society of Actuaries. The 100th anniversary of the actuarial profession in America was felt to be a good time to review various aspects of the profession. This monograph deals with the significant mortality tables that have been used by members of the Society in the last 100 years.

Chapter I presents general statistics on mortality in the United States. Insurance mortality tables are drawn from selected portions of the population, so the population mortality rates present a useful backdrop for the discussion of insurance company mortality tables.

Chapter II discusses the major statutory mortality tables that have been in use in the United States in the last century. By reference to "use", rather than "publication", the seminal American Experience table could be included.

Chapter III discusses the shape and trend of mortality experience in the United States. This chapter includes a discussion of the applicability of the various "Laws of Mortality" over the last 100 years.

The author wishes to thank a number of people who provided their kind assistance.

Dan Case and Regina Van Valkenburgh provided free and frequent access to the libraries of the American Council on Life Insurance and of the Office of the Actuary of the Treasury Department, respectively. Toni Hustead and her staff at the Office of the Actuary of the Department of Defense compiled the mortality rates for all of the tables in this study.

As always, the staff of the Society of Actuaries was extremely helpful. Donna Richardson provided invaluable assistance in obtaining needed materials and references. Jack Luff and Mark Doherty provided encouragement as well as review and advice.

Robert J. Myers provided extensive information on the United States censuses. His articles, some jointly with Francisco Bayo, were the basis for most of Chapter I. And he was kind enough to provide copies of the older census tables, as well as his thorough comments on the draft of the paper.

Particular acknowledgement is given to the historical series of mortality table compilations begun by Nelson and Warren; and continued by Tillinghast. According to Don Warren, the series started in the 1940s as a Christmas present for clients of Nelson and Warren. It turned out to be a very popular item and the periodic updates have kept it a current and complete compilation and explanation of mortality tables. The 1987 version of *Principal Mortality Tables OLD and NEW* was an invaluable guide to and summary of the primary tables used by insurance companies in the United States as well as a single source for the life expectancies for mortality tables reviewed in this paper. Carol Reynolds of Tillinghast provided a copy of the most recent version of the series and invaluable assistance in interpreting the series.

Reviewers of the paper included Tom Bowles, Don Warren, Rick Foster, Cecil Nesbitt, Robert Johansen, Lindsay Malkiewich, Duane Kidwell and Stanley Hill.

Beatrice Locher of Hay/Huggins Company, Incorporated and Judy Yore and Cherie Harrold of the Society of Actuaries provided assistance in preparing the final document for publication.

I. MORTALITY IN THE UNITED STATES

This chapter presents the history of mortality for the United States population as a framework for the discussion of the mortality tables used by the actuarial profession in the United States. Population data have been gathered in the United States since 1790. Beginning in 1850, deaths in Massachusetts were matched against population data to determine the rates of mortality by age and sex. At the time of the 1900 census, mortality measurement was extended to the ten states, and the District of Columbia, which had become designated as Death Registration States. A state was admitted as a Death Registration State after demonstrating that complete records of deaths were kept. By 1930, all states had achieved this status and were included in the measurement of mortality in the United States.

A life table has been constructed from data centering on each of the censuses. For instance, the 1979-1981 United States Life Table was based on the 1980 census, with appropriate adjustment, and deaths from 1979, 1980, and 1981. The information on the United States Life Tables is largely drawn from "United States Life Tables for 1979-81" by Myers and Bayo.[1] This is the latest in a series of papers on the decennial life table. The earlier papers were by Myers.

Note that the rate of mortality is the probability that an individual will die in the next year. For instance, a rate of mortality of .01 at age 60 means that there is a one percent chance that a person who has just reached age 60 will die before his 61st birthday.

TRENDS IN RATES OF MORTALITY

The first part of the twentieth century saw rapid improvements in mortality at the younger ages and in the last 40 years mortality has improved at all ages. Charts I.1.1 through I.2.2 show the rate of improvement in mortality at every tenth age for white males and females for alternate censuses from 1900 through 1980. These tables were used because data for white males and females are available from 1900 through 1980.

The mortality rates for children dropped by more than 90% from 1900 through 1980 with significant decreases in each 20 year period. The male mortality rates over age 60 dropped by about 30% since 1900 with three-fourths of that decrease occurring after 1940. Female mortality improvement was significantly greater than for males with the lowest improvement being 40% at age 90.

Charts I.1.1 and I.1.2 show that there have been some important exceptions to the steady improvement in mortality for white males. Between 1920 and 1940 there was little or no improvement in mortality for white males age 50 and over. The

Chart I.1.1
White Male Mortality Rates
U.S. Life Tables 1900 to 1980

Deaths in Year Per 10,000 Alive

Year of Census

AGE	1900	1920	1940	1960	1980
0	1335	803	481	259	123
10	27	21	10	4	2
20	59	43	21	16	18
30	80	57	28	16	17
40	106	75	51	33	26
50	154	117	116	96	71
60	286	246	255	227	176
70	589	546	545	487	415
80	1335	1197	1247	1073	910
90	2628	2381	2489	2360	1906

Chart I.1.2
White Male Mortality Rates
U.S. Life Tables 1900 to 1980

Percent Decrease In Death Rate

AGE	1900 to 1920	1920 to 1940	1940 to 1960	1960 to 1980	1900 to 1980
0	39.9%	40.0%	46.1%	52.5%	90.8%
10	23.0	52.6	58.0	54.8	93.1
20	28.1	50.4	25.0	-10.1	70.5
30	28.3	51.3	44.1	-6.4	79.2
40	29.2	31.6	35.3	21.4	75.4
50	23.6	1.6	17.3	26.1	54.1
60	13.9	-3.5	10.9	22.4	38.4
70	7.3	0.2	10.7	14.8	29.6
80	10.3	-4.2	13.9	15.2	31.9
90	9.4	-4.6	5.2	19.2	27.5

Chart I.2.1
White Female Mortality Rates
U.S. Life Tables 1900 to 1980

Deaths In Year Per 10,000 Alive

Year of Census

AGE	1900	1920	1940	1960	1980
0	1,106	639	379	196	97
10	25	18	11	3	2
20	55	43	14	6	6
30	77	69	22	9	7
40	93	68	37	19	14
50	134	107	76	47	38
60	251	217	171	109	89
70	537	502	423	284	209
80	1,212	1,134	1,082	821	559
90	2,453	2,306	2,314	2,256	1,483

Chart I.2.2
White Female Mortality Rates
U.S. Life Tables 1900 to 1980

Percent Decrease In Death Rate

AGE	1900 to 1920	1920 to 1940	1940 to 1960	1960 to 1980	1900 to 1980
0	42.2%	40.7%	48.2%	50.9%	91.3%
10	27.2	38.5	74.5	39.3	93.1
20	21.8	66.5	61.4	0.0	89.9
30	10.2	68.3	61.4	23.5	91.6
40	27.4	45.6	48.4	24.7	84.6
50	20.2	28.6	37.9	20.5	71.9
60	13.3	21.1	36.5	18.3	64.5
70	6.4	15.7	33.0	26.2	61.0
80	6.4	4.6	24.1	31.9	53.9
90	6.0	-0.3	2.5	34.3	39.5

most significant improvement for most ages was between 1960 and 1980. However, the rate of mortality for young men actually increased in that period.

The differences in rates of improvement by age and period result from the different histories of improving treatment for acute and chronic diseases causing death. In the early part of the twentieth century, the acute diseases accounted for a large proportion of deaths. Efforts in the early part of the twentieth century were largely focused on improvements in public health that greatly reduced the risk from contagious diseases. The risk from contagious diseases dropped even more sharply with the widespread use of antibiotics in the 1940s.

As the risk from contagious diseases was reduced, mortality improved at all ages, but at the older ages the improvement was largely offset by the fact that there was not a significant reduction in mortality from chronic diseases. In the last 40 years, improvement in mortality from all causes has resulted in significant improvement at all ages.

Charts I.3.1 and I.3.2 show the ten leading causes of death in 1900 and 1985 as measured by the Public Health Service.[2] The three leading causes in 1900 (tuberculosis, pneumonia, and diarrhea and enteritis) accounted for a third of the deaths. By 1985, the three leading causes were chronic

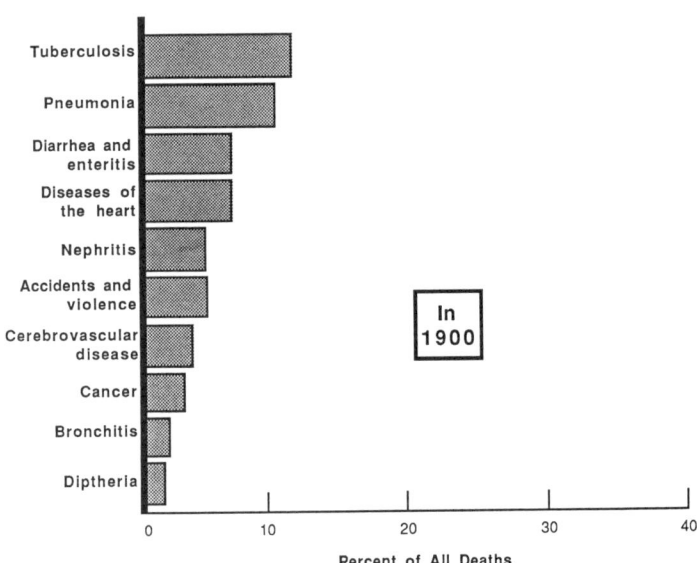

Chart I.3.1
The Ten Leading Causes of Death in 1900

Source: Public Health Service

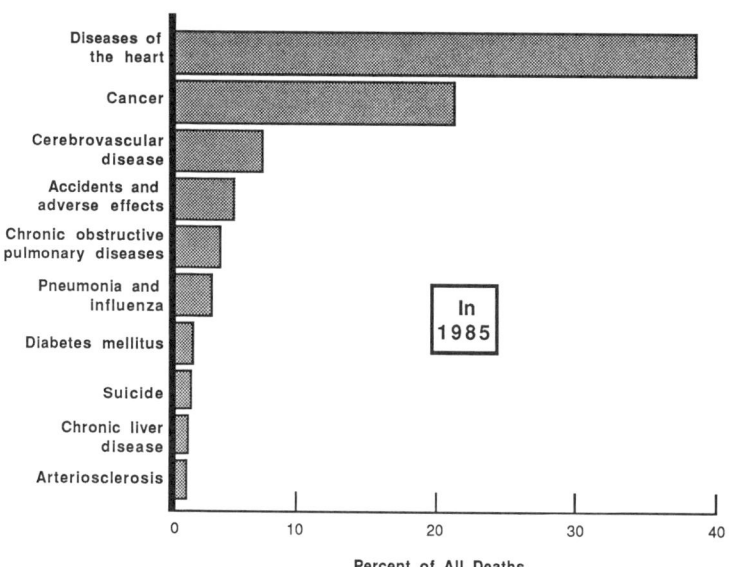

Chart I.3.2
The Ten Leading Causes of Death in 1985

Source: Public Health Service

diseases (diseases of the heart, cancer, and cerebrovascular disease), which accounted for two-thirds of all deaths. Note that the causes of death were more evenly distributed in 1900 than in 1985.

Chart I.4 shows the life expectancy at birth by sex as measured in each year from 1900 through 1987. These tables are derived from an analysis by the Social Security Administration and include mortality for all races.[3] The Social Security Administration presented data for years between the decennial censuses from abridged life tables for those years, based on recorded deaths and estimated populations.

If small year-to-year fluctuations are ignored, there has been a steady improvement in mortality observed in the United States Life Tables with the notable exception of 1917 and 1918. In 1918, the life expectancy dropped by seven years. By 1919, the life expectancy had recovered and continued its climb to the present level. The drop in 1917 and 1918 was attributable to the influenza epidemic of those years.

MORTALITY FROM BIRTH TO AGE 35

Charts I.5 through I.7 show the 1979-81 Life Table mortality rates for white males and females. The charts show three distinct patterns of mortality. The first is a very low level before age 35

This chart, I.4, should have appeared after page 10. However, it was inadvertently omitted in the printing process.

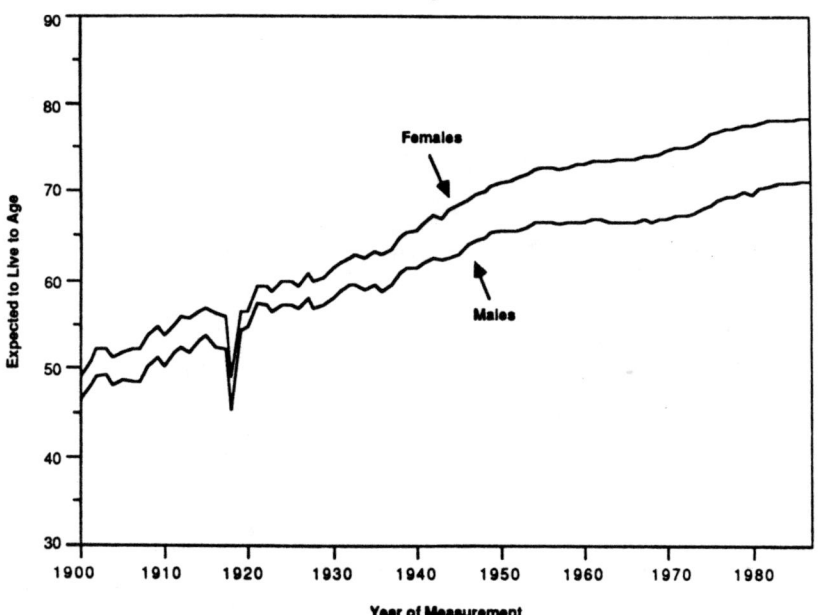

**Chart I.4
Expectation of Life at Birth
U.S. Population**

Source: Social Security Administration

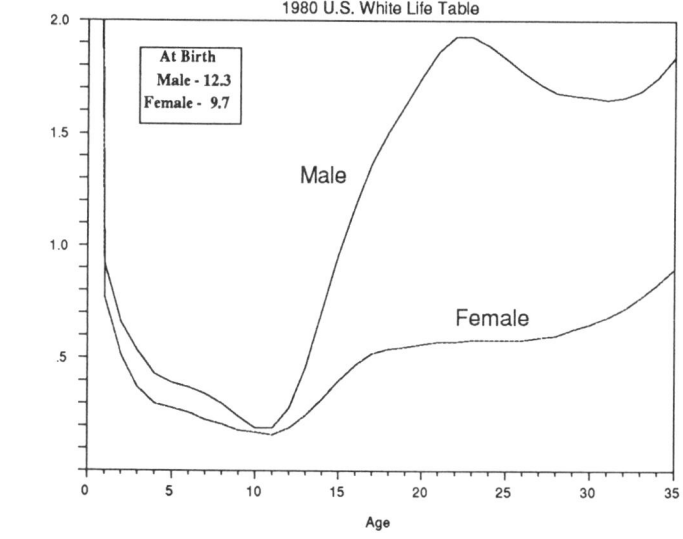

with fluctuations that are not directly correlated with age. The second is a geometric pattern of increases from the thirties to the seventies. The third is a reduced rate of increase as the rates approach their highest level.

The rate of mortality is around 10 deaths in the first year of life per 1,000 births dropping rapidly to under one death per 1,000 in the second year of life. The mortality rate hits its lowest point at 0.2 per 1,000 around age 10 and then begins a largely uninterrupted climb with the exception of a dip in the rate of mortality for males in their late twenties. The male mortality rate hits a temporary peak at 1.9 per 1,000 at age 22 and drops to 1.7 per 1,000 at age 31.

The male and female rates are fairly close together until the teenage years, but then begin to diverge as the higher accidental death rate for young men drives up the mortality for males in their twenties. The female mortality rate increases to 0.4 per 1,000 in the late teens and then climbs slowly to 0.7 per 1,000 by age 30.

The very low rates of mortality for children around age 10 probably are close to the lowest accidental mortality rate that can be achieved in an industrial society. The increase in the teens, especially for males, reflects the increased risk from automobiles and other societal factors as children become adults. Two-thirds of the deaths for white males between the ages of 15 and 24 are from accidents, homicide or suicide. Trends in deaths from these three causes explain the increase in male mortality at the younger ages in recent years.

MORTALITY FROM AGE 35 TO AGE 70

As shown in Chart I.6, soon after age 35, a steady geometric rate of increase takes over the mortality curve. In the 1979-81 Life Tables, the rate of increase from one age to the next is around ten percent beginning at age 35 for females and age 41 for males. This increase factor is fairly constant until the oldest ages when the rate of increase begins to slow. This characteristic of a geometric growth for a large portion of the table has been observed from the earliest scientifically constructed tables.

As will be discussed in Chapter III, this geometric rate of increase in mortality is the basis for the laws of mortality proposed by Gompertz and Makeham. However, the mortality rates before age 35 and at the oldest ages do not follow the same pattern of a constant rate of increase.

The ratio of female to male mortality is lowest in the twenties when female rates are a third of male rates. By age 35, the female rates are around half of the male rates, and they stay at that relative position until age 70. The geometric growth in the female rates from one age to the

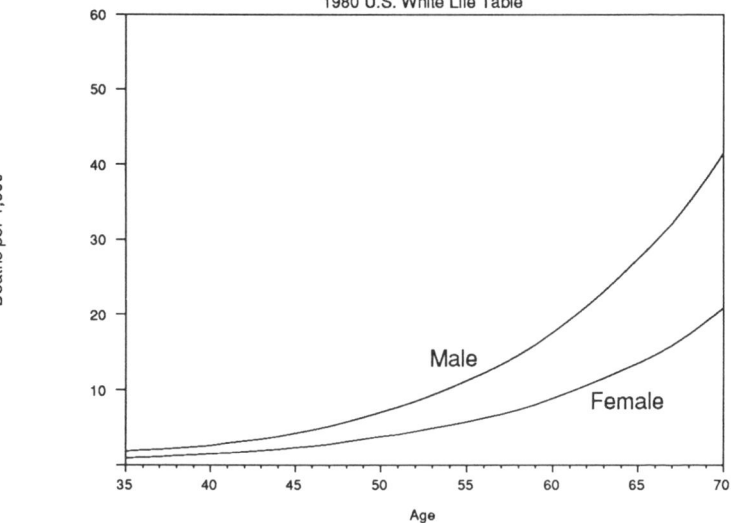

next stays at around 10% until age 90, but the rate of growth in the male rates begins to drop at age 60. Since the female rate grows faster than the male rate after age 60, the difference in mortality diminishes with age.

MORTALITY AFTER AGE 70

Chart I.7 shows the mortality rates after age 70. The rate of increase in the 1979-81 Life Table mortality rates begins to drop below 10% around age 60 for males and age 90 for females. Thereafter, the rate of growth in the mortality curve begins to decline. The rate of increase for males continues at 8% or more through age 86 and then declines further. By age 100, the rate of increase for both males and females is less than 5% a year. A question that has not yet been satisfactorily answered is whether the mortality rate eventually levels off, or if it continues to increase at all ages, but at progressively slower rates.

Studies of mortality at the oldest ages are inhibited by two problems. First, even in a very large population there are few people still alive at the very old ages, so mortality rates have much less statistical significance than at the younger ages. Second, people tend to exaggerate their ages as they approach the centenarian point. Because of these problems, even mortality tables based on the total United States population have to be estimated at the oldest ages. These esti-

Chart I.7

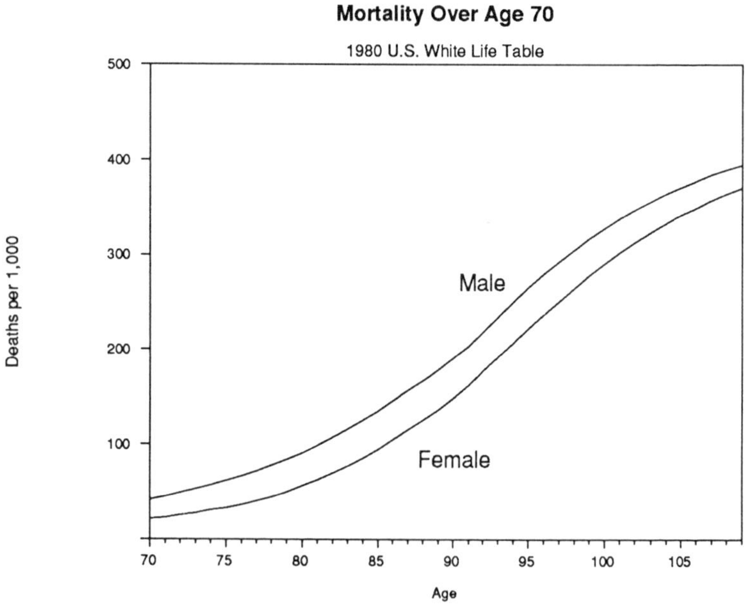

Mortality Over Age 70
1980 U.S. White Life Table
Deaths per 1,000
500
400
300
200
100
Male
Female
70
75
80
85
90
95
100
105
Age

mates at the oldest ages are usually based on extrapolations from younger ages and information from detailed studies of mortality from data sources that are known to be more reliable than census data at the oldest ages.

In one such detailed study, Francisco Bayo and Joseph Faber followed the experience for the earliest Social Security beneficiaries.[4] These "charter" OASDI beneficiaries were known to be born between 1872 and 1875 and were the initial recipients of benefits from Social Security in 1940. Therefore, the records on these individuals were very good. The oldest male died at age 107 and the oldest female at age 105. Since females have a greater life expectancy than males, it would be expected that there would be more females at the very oldest ages in any given population. However, females were a relatively small portion of people working in the 1930s, and hence few were eligible for retirement benefits in 1940. Therefore, Bayo and Faber's study contains a lower proportion of females than there are in the entire population.

Bayo and Faber concluded that the rate of increase in the mortality curve slowed after age 85, but the evidence from the study could support either of two hypotheses about the ultimate pattern of mortality: either the rate becomes level at a certain age, or it continues to increase, but at a much lower rate than before age 85.

Lew and Garfinkel analyzed the mortality rates from a major epidemiologic study of over one million people conducted by the American Cancer Society beginning in 1959.[5] The oldest male in the study died at age 109. Five females survived to age 110 and the oldest died at age 114. The observed death rates first exceeded 33% at age 97 for males and age 101 for females. The rates fluctuated between 28% and 44% for most ages after that point except for ages at which there were fewer than ten observations.

The conclusion to be drawn from these two studies is that the rate of mortality at the oldest ages probably does not exceed 400 to 500 out of every 1,000 people alive at the beginning of the year. Chart I.7 shows that the rates of mortality from the 1979-81 life table were approaching an ultimate rate at those levels after age 100.

LIFE EXPECTANCY IN THE TWENTIETH CENTURY

Charts I.8 and I.9 show the life expectancies for white males at ages 20 and 60 associated with each census of the United States since 1900. The charts show the expected number of years of life for individuals who have already attained age 20 or 60. For instance, in 1980, a white male age 60 could have expected to live for 16 more years. These charts will be the basis for comparison of tables from insurance company experience.

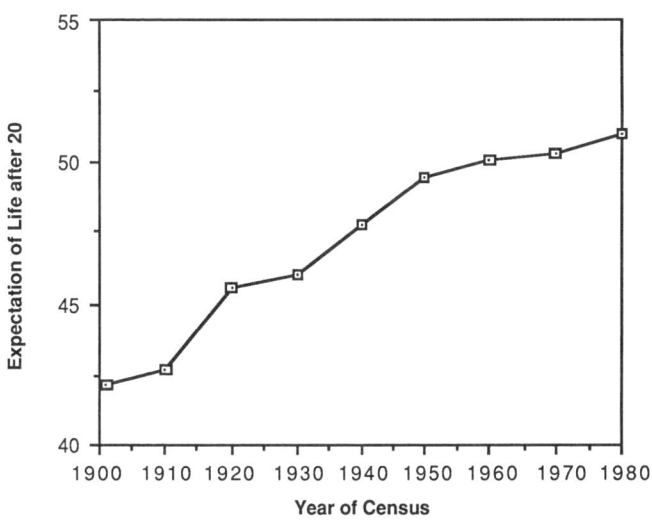

**Chart I.8
Expectation of Life at Age 20
United States Life Tables-White Males**

**Chart I.9
Expectation of Life at Age 60
United States Life Tables-White Males**

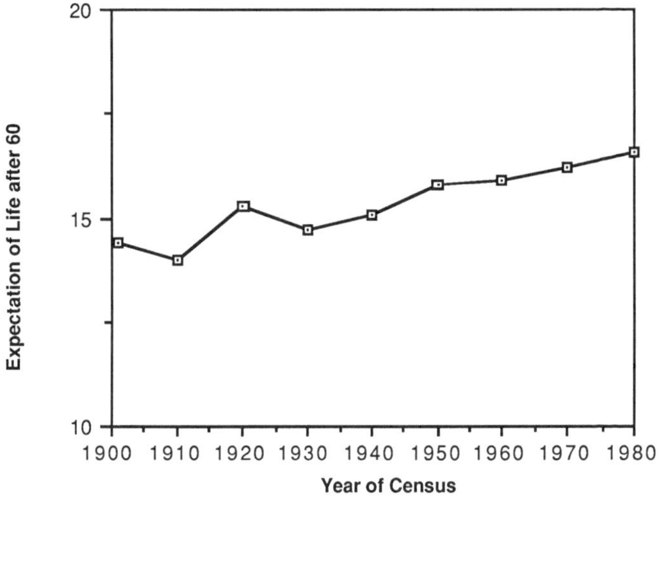

The life expectancies at age 20 are appropriate for comparison to life insurance mortality tables. Only a small portion of the insurance in force is issued to people under age 20, so earlier ages are usually not important in determining mortality for most life insurance policies. The life expectancies at age 60 are appropriate for comparison to annuity mortality tables, since most annuities start after age 60.

II. MORTALITY TABLES USED BY ACTUARIES IN THE UNITED STATES

The tables described in this chapter are only a small number of the tables that have been and are being used by actuaries in the United States. The Tillinghast approach[6] of reporting on the "principal" mortality tables has been adopted. Most of these are tables that have been adopted by states for use in performing company valuations for official financial statements. A primary attribute of valuation tables is that they must predict the financial situation of an insurance plan with a margin for safety. Therefore, an official valuation table usually is based on recent experience at the time of publication with a margin for safety.

Statutory tables should provide reasonably safe reserves for all companies. Therefore, a life insurance table should predict mortality that is high enough to cover the great majority of companies. Companies with worse experience would be expected to strengthen the table for their purpose.

The paper presenting the Commissioners 1980 Standard Ordinary Mortality Table (1980 CSO) states that the tables "would be inappropriate for the pricing of individual ordinary insurance. Most major life insurance companies would rely on their own recent mortality experience for determining guaranteed gross premiums on nonparticipating insurance or for the setting of dividend scales on participating insurance."[7]

TYPES OF MORTALITY TABLES

Chart II.1 shows the genealogy of the principal mortality tables developed from insurance in force in the United States.

The earliest tables were used for all branches of insurance. However, in the first two decades of the Actuarial Society of America, major segments of the industry decided that the general mortality tables were not appropriate for their specific lines of business. The first split was between life insurance and annuity tables with the McClintock table published in 1899. A second split occurred with the first industrial insurance table in 1906.

Both the insurance and annuity families of tables have since split to produce separate tables for individual and group business. The first group life insurance table was Cammack's table of 1927. A separate series of group annuity tables began with the Group Annuity Table for 1951 (1951 Ga).

Different mortality tables are now used by different segments of the insurance industry. Current tables include the 1980 CSO for individual life insurance, the Commissioners 1960 Standard Group Mortality Table (1960 CSG) for group life insurance, the 1983 Individual Annuity Mortality Table (Table a) for individual annuities, the 1983

Chart II.1

**Principal United States
Insurance Company Mortality Tables**

Year Published

```
1865 ─┤              American Experience
                    /        |        \
                   /         |         \
1885 ─┤           /          |          \
                 /           |           \
                /            |            \
               /             |             \
          McClintock         |              \
1905 ─┤       |              |          Standard
              |              |          Industrial
         American            |              |
         Annuitants      American           |
              |          Men                |
1925 ─┤       |              |              |
         Combined            |     Cammack  |
         Annuity             |        |     |
              1937        1941              1941
              SA          CSO               SI
1945 ─┤      / |             |               |
         1951 1949           |               |
         GAM  SA             |               |
                          1958     1960      |
                          CSO      CSG     1961
1965 ─┤       |    |          |              SI
            1971  1971        |
            GAM   IAM         |
           /  \    |          |
        UP 84 1983 1983     1980
              GAM  IAM      CSO
1985 ─┤
```

Annuity	Insurance
Group	Individual	Group	Industrial

Line of Business

25

Group Annuity Mortality Table (1983 GAM) for insured pensions, and the UP-1984 table for uninsured pensions.

The margin for safety in statutory mortality tables works in opposite directions for life insurance and annuities. A safety margin is built into life insurance tables by increasing the rates of mortality. The margin is built into annuity tables by reducing the rates of mortality (i.e., increasing the expected probability of living and, therefore, collecting benefits).

Chart II.2 illustrates why different approaches are taken to provide a safety margin for annuities and life insurance. If the rates predict that 50 out of 1,000 policyholders will die, but only 45 of 1,000 die, the insured group will show a ten percent gain. However, more annuity benefits than expected will be paid since there are more policyholders alive, and therefore receiving benefits, than were expected. Using the simplifying assumption that all deaths occur at the beginning of the year, the annuity payments will be $50,000 more than expected each year. The mortality table that provides safety for life insurance creates losses for annuities.

Chart II.2

BENEFITS TO 1,000 POLICYHOLDERS

Expected Deaths = 50

Actual Deaths = 45

INSURANCE BENEFITS
($100,000 Face Amount)

Expected Benefit = $5,000,000 for 50 deaths
Actual Benefit   = 4,500,000 for 45 deaths

Gain $ 500,000

ANNUITY PAYMENTS
($10,000 a Year)

Expected Benefit = $9,500,000 for 950 alive
Actual Benefit   = 9,550,000 for 955 alive

Annual Loss $ 50,000

The secular improvement in mortality in the last century thus has had very different implications for life insurance and annuities. Even if a mortality table has no specific margin for safety, a margin for insurance will develop as mortality improves. On the other hand, a margin for safety in a table for annuities will gradually disappear as mortality improves.

The result is that actuaries who develop tables for annuities are very concerned about trends in mortality and usually suggest projection of mortality improvement as a margin against adverse experience. But, actuaries who develop tables for insurance do not project the mortality improvement because any reduction in mortality will increase the safety margin of the table.

The different focus of the developers of life insurance and annuity tables can be seen in two papers in the same volume of the *Transactions of the Society of Actuaries*. The paper describing the 1980 CSO uses 1970 to 1975 experience without adjustment and does not even discuss the desirability or need to project experience. (*TSA*, V.33, 617-666) The paper describing the 1983 Individual Annuity Mortality Table explains how the underlying data were projected forward to represent experience in 1983 and includes a detailed presentation and discussion of factors that the actuary might use to project the experience into the future. A full third of the paper is concerned with projections.[8]

In fact, the development of the 1983 GAM Table took this process one step further. Projection techniques were the principal means of developing this new standard. (*TSA*, V.35, 859-899)

The different needs for safety margins also help

to explain why separate male and female tables were used for annuities long before they were used in life insurance tables. Use of a male table for females, with its higher rate of mortality, will create a margin for safety for life insurance, but losses for annuities. The first annuity table prepared in the United States, McClintock's, adopted the European approach of using different male and female tables. However, the statutory individual life insurance tables were on a combined basis until the latest (1980) CSO table, although age setbacks had often been used for female rates and reserves.

Other mortality tables for specific lines of insurance have been developed when a segment of the insurance industry has realized that their mortality is significantly different from that of the traditional life insurance policies. One family of tables that was once very important was for industrial life insurance which was sold for weekly premiums to people who were of the "industrial" class. Separate tables were needed because the mortality for industrial policyholders would be expected to be higher than for traditional life insurance policyholders.

Soon after insurance began to be issued to groups as well as individuals, actuaries examined group mortality to see if it differed from insurance issued on an individual basis. There were two underwriting differences that were expected to lead to different patterns of mortality. First, the insurer usually had to accept all members of the group, so some individuals who were uninsurable for individual policies would be covered in groups.

On the other hand, the group was usually a working population so the average person in the group could be expected to be healthier than the average individual applying for insurance. Group annuities also differed from individual annuities because of the need to provide values at the younger ages. Group annuities are usually purchased during the working life while individual annuities are usually purchased at the time the annuity begins.

BRITISH MORTALITY TABLES USED IN THE UNITED STATES

When the Actuarial Society of America was founded, four British tables were used extensively by actuaries in the United States. These were the Northampton, Carlisle, Combined Experience, and Healthy Male (H^m) Tables. [9]

The earliest of the four was the Northampton Table. This table was derived by Dr. Richard Price from records maintained by the parish of All Saints in the town of Northampton between 1735 and 1780. A valid complete mortality table could be derived from parish records in eighteenth century England since there was little migration between towns, and almost all residents belonged to the Church of England. Nevertheless, there was some error in measurement "caused almost entirely by deaths among the Dissenters." (Elston, *Sources*,6)

The Carlisle Table of Mortality was constructed by Joshua Milne from the registers of deaths and censuses in two parishes in Carlisle. Deaths that occurred between 1779 and 1787 were compared to censuses performed in 1780 and 1787.

The Combined Experience Table (also known as the Actuaries' Table) was based on experience of the policyholders of 17 life companies in Great Britain in the 1830s. The table was constructed by tracking information on over 80,000 policies through 1837. The table was adopted as the official valuation basis by the state of Massachusetts and was commonly used by insurance companies in the United States.

The Healthy Male (H^m) Table was used by actuaries in the United States, but was not adopted as a statutory basis. The table was one of several derived by the Institute of Actuaries in 1862 from 160,000 policyholders of 20 British companies.

AMERICAN EXPERIENCE TABLE

The American Experience Table holds a unique position in the history of mortality tables. It was the first widely-used table based on life insurance mortality experience in the United States. The first mortality table based on United States experience was constructed by Professor Wigglesworth in 1789. The Wigglesworth table, however, was based on population records, not insurance company records. (Elston, *Sources*,35) In its early years, it was the mortality basis for all lines of insurance and annuities. Perhaps most remarkably, the American Experience Table was used as the primary statutory table for individual insurance policies from its introduction in 1868 until it was replaced by the 1941 CSO Table beginning in 1948. Since policies issued under the American Experience basis continued to be valued on that table after 1948, the American Experience Table was actually used for more than a century. By the end of that hundred year period, the life expectancy of the general population at birth was 25 years longer than that based on the American Experience Table.

The table was the work of one man, Sheppard Homans, and was based on mortality experience of the Mutual Life Insurance Company of New York. Most of what is known about the table comes from a speech by Homans after the first dinner of the Actuarial Society of America at the Astor Hotel in New York on April 25, 1889.[10]

Homans stated that, while the table was based on the experience of the Mutual Life, he did not view it as an accurate representation of the experience of that company. Elston believed that the table was based on the experience of the Mutual Life from 1843 to 1860, and that Homans probably added a safety margin since he did state that he removed the effect of medical selection. Homans did not use the name "American Experience," that later became attached to the table. He described the development of the table as follows:

> "The result was that after I had collated the experience of the Mutual Life I drew a curve representing the approximate rates of mortality at different ages; and then found, by a simple method of adjustment, the rates of mortality now called 'the American Experience Table'..." (Homans, *Response*, 33)

INSURANCE TABLES

The American Experience Table, and the British tables developed from insurance experience, were derived by examining the experience of traditional individual life insurance policies. The family of individual life insurance tables extends through the 1980 CSO. Group insurance tables were first differentiated from individual insurance tables with Cammack's tables of 1927.

Individual Insurance

The Actuarial Society of America and the American Institute of Actuaries jointly produced a new table for general use as a life insurance valuation standard in 1918. This table, the American Men Table, was based on the experience of 59 life insurance companies from 1900 through 1914. The ultimate male mortality table ($AM^{(5)}$) since it excluded experience for the first five years after issue, was widely used by insurance companies to set rates. It was not accepted as the valuation standard for individual insurance.

The $AM^{(5)}$ Table was developed to meet a need for a new mortality table, but the timing of its publication in 1918 was not propitious. The profession had been prepared to replace the aging American Experience Table, but the unexpectedly high levels of mortality from the influenza epidemic and World War I caused the leading actuaries to agree that the profession should stick with a table that was overly safe in case wars and epidemics continued to appear.[11]

Even as late as the 1930s, the insurance companies and the Insurance Commissioners were not overly concerned with the currency of the American Experience Table since the margin for safety grew as mortality improved. However, critics outside of the insurance industry expressed concern about the appropriateness of premiums based on an outdated table. The Commissioners did not agree with the public criticism "that insurance companies are receiving unconscionable profits through its use,"[12] but they recognized the adverse public relations aspect of the use of such an old and conservative table and asked the profession to develop a new table.

The Commissioner's 1941 Standard Ordinary Table was based on the experience of 16 life insurance companies in the United States and Canada under their policies from 1931 through 1940. The table was graduated and loaded to provide a table with smooth rates that had a margin for safety. These two operations produced a table of rates that were substantially higher than the underlying experience. Therefore, the 1941 CSO Table was accompanied by a table to be used for comparison of actual underlying experience. Tables based on underlying experience before addition of margins are called "basic" tables.

The next in the series of individual life insurance tables was the 1958 CSO.[13] The 1958 CSO, and the accompanying basic table, were based on intercompany experience between 1950 and 1954. A "dip" in the underlying experience at ages 27 to 32 was removed to avoid an interruption in the pattern of increasing mortality. The observed rates were loaded for safety and graduated to produce the 1958 CSO Table. The final rates were adjusted so that they would not exceed the mortality rates from the 1949-51 United States Life Table for White Males. This last step was taken for public relations purposes since it was believed that it would be difficult to explain why insurance company rates were higher than general population rates.

As with the 1941 CSO, a basic table showing the underlying experience was prepared. The 1958 Basic Table was produced from the 1958 CSO by removing the margins. By 1958, females still represented a small, although growing, segment of life insurance experience. Therefore, the table was based on all experience and presented as a male table. Since the proportion of females was increasing, and since it was becoming the practice to charge lower rates to females of the same age as males, this was the last insurance table to be on a combined basis. Reserves for female insurance policies after 1958 were often based on an age setback of the male 1958 CSO rates.

The 1958 Commissioners Extended Term Mortality Table was developed as part of the 1958 Table work. It included a loading of the greater of 0.75 deaths per 1,000 or 30% to the rates in the 1958 CSO Table. This table was to replace the use of 130% of the 1941 CSO Table in the valuation of the extended term benefit.

The 1958 CSO was followed by the 1980 CSO and 1980 basic tables based on 1970 through 1975 insurance company experience. (*TSA*, V.33, 618-619) The 1980 Commissioners Extended Term Table was developed from the 1980 CSO Table in the same fashion as the 1958 CET Table had been developed from the 1958 CSO Table. These tables have been used as a valuation standard for new business since 1981. There are six important differences between the methods used to develop the 1958 and 1980 mortality tables.

- The 1980 tables included policies issued on both medical and non-medical bases since it was becoming less and less common to use medical underwriting.

- Separate 1980 CSO Tables were prepared for males and females. The 1958 Table had been developed from combined experience but recommended for males.

- The "dip" in mortality rates from male ages 22 to 32 was reflected in the 1980 CSO table although a similar dip had been smoothed out in the 1958 CSO Table.

- The Basic Table was constructed first, and then loaded, to produce the 1980 CSO Table. The 1958 Basic Table had been produced by removing the margin from the 1958 CSO Table.

- Select factors for each of the first ten policy years were developed for use with the 1980 CSO Table. No select factors were developed for the 1958 CSO Table.

- Following the development of the 1980 CSO Tables, smoker and non-smoker scaling factors were developed for use with these tables. This was the first recognition of smoking status in valuation tables.

The Society of Actuaries collects data and issues annual reports of intercompany mortality under ordinary life insurance policies. From time to time, "basic tables" are constructed from this data and become the basis that is used for comparisons in subsequent yearly studies. The 1965-70 and 1975-80 Basic Tables[14] are the latest in this series.

These tables reflect life company operations, in particular, pricing or premium setting. As such, they are constructed on a "select and ultimate" basis. Since newly issued policies have been underwritten, the lives they cover are classified as being in good health. A mortality table reflecting this very good experience in the first policy year after issue is constructed. The effect of underwriting, or selection, wears off as time passes and mortality tables for each policy year are constructed reflecting this progressively higher mortality. Ultimately, the effects of selection are negligable and the experience is combined into a single set of values by attained age. Currently, a fifteen year select period is typically used, but different values may be used for special purposes and have been used in the past.

Insurance company operations are concerned with

equity among different underwriting classes of insured persons. The studies of the Society mirror these concerns to the extent it is practical. In addition to age, duration and gender distinctions, distinctions are also made by type of underwriting (medical, paramedical and nonmedical) and smoking status (smoker, non-smoker and unknown). Special studies also provide information on substandard issues and additional benefits.

The unit of measurement for these studies is generally the amount of insurance, rather than the number of policies. This weighs the mortality rates by size of policy. The result is considered to be a better measure of the financial effect of the experience.

These tables and studies are published in the *Reports* volumes of the Society, the most recent of which is the 1984 *Reports*.

Group Insurance

By the 1920s, insurance industry actuaries and regulators had decided that a specific mortality table was needed for group insurance. Actuaries were concerned that reserve factors for individual insurance were not appropriate for group insurance. However, the primary concern was that group insurance companies were driven by competitive pressures to set group premium rates that were too low. Therefore, a group insurance mortality table was needed to establish minimum group insurance rates. The Superintendent of Insurance for the state of New York first regulated group insurance in 1926 because of his "concern...over the intense competition for new business which he feared would be harmful to the companies and demoralizing to the then infant group insurance."[15]

This concern encouraged group insurance actuaries to develop a separate table in 1927. However, until 1960, the group insurance statutes were based on individual life insurance tables. Group insurance statutes initially specified use of the $AM^{(5)}$ Table. The $AM^{(5)}$ Table was replaced with the 1941 CSO in the 1950s. The first specific group insurance table used in statutes was the Commissioners 1960 Standard Group Mortality Table.

The first tables developed specifically for group insurance were the two Cammack Mortality Tables[16] based on the experience of six American and Canadian companies from 1913 to 1926. These tables were widely used in the insurance industry even though they were not adopted as statutory tables by the state commissioners. One of the tables provided rates based on general experience and the other on the experience of "clerical" employees. The latter table became known as the Cammack Clerical Table and was widely used for group insurance rates and reserves. The rates were the sum of mortality and disability rates. This was done because employees who became disabled typically received the face amount of insurance after a specified period of disability, such as six months. Therefore, disability had almost the same financial impact on the insurance company as death.

The current, and only other, table developed from group life insurance experience was the Commissioners 1960 Standard Group Mortality Table. This table was based on intercompany insured experience from 1950 through 1958. A safety margin was added and the table was extended before and after the working ages by using ratios to mortality rates from the 1958 CSO Table. A 1960 Basic Group Table was constructed by removing the margins and making other adjustments.[17] The table is used for premium setting only.

ANNUITY TABLES

Individual Annuities

Since 1899, a distinct family of tables has been used for annuities. The first was McClintock's Table published in *TASA VI*.[18] Emory McClintock introduced his table by noting that "It has appeared to me that there is no existing mortality table which can be used with satisfaction in the computation of reserves upon life annuities" (pg 13). McClintock's Table was loosely based on earlier data compiled by Rufus W. Weeks from experience of fifteen American companies on their annuity policies before 1892. McClintock reduced the experience rates to produce a margin for safety and graduated the table by a Makeham formula. He adopted the European practice of producing separate annuity tables for males and females. McClintock's Table was adopted by New York and several other states as the standard table for annuity valuations.

The next annuity table in general use was the American Annuitants Table derived by Dr. Arthur Hunter from the experience of 20 American companies on issues prior to 1917 examined through 1918.[19] Hunter noted that improvements in health and sanitary conditions might improve mortality, but he did not suggest a specific method to allow for such improvement.

The next in the series was the 1937 Standard Annuity Table.[20] In his paper presenting the table, Frank Kineke noted that the practice was to allow for improvement in mortality for annuities by "rating down" earlier tables. The practice of rating down is now called "setting back." Setbacks are used to reduce the mortality rates and, thereby, build a margin into the resulting reserve levels. A setback means that all rates from the original table are assigned to an age n years older to produce the new table. If, for instance, the mortality rate at age 60 is .05 and the rate at 61 is .055, a new table with a setback of one year will use the .05 rate at 61 and the

.055 rate at 62. However, Kineke expressed concern that a rating down that would be appropriate for one span of ages would not be valid at other ages because of the different tilts in different parts of the mortality curve. This suggested the need for a new table that would reflect current mortality at all ages. The 1937 Standard Annuity Table was not, however, based on a new study of mortality. The table was largely based on a two-year setback of the American Annuitants Table at the older ages.

The 1949 Standard Annuity Table (a-1949) was the first in a series of individual annuity tables that was presented as a "basic" table which would be adjusted by a projection scale to be appropriate for the specific year of valuation. The older ages were based on a study of annuity experience from 1941 through 1946. This experience was blended with group annuity experience below age 55 for males and 50 for females. The resulting table was projected forward to represent experience in 1949.

McClintock had observed that the great progress in medicine and hygiene made it necessary to use recent experience and to add margins. However, neither he nor the other writers before 1949 had suggested methods for keeping mortality rates current. Jenkins and Lew presented two projection scales, A and B, which could be used to project the a-1949 table to any future year.[21] Authors of later annuity tables followed this approach of using letters to identify their recommended projection factors.

The next annuity table was the 1955 American Annuity Table.[22] The table was specifically developed for use in setting rates for annuity settlement options that can be purchased with the proceeds of a life insurance policy. Settlement options had originally been introduced as an alternative to the payment of insurance proceeds in a lump-sum by permitting the beneficiary to elect to receive benefits as an annuity. It had been expected that few beneficiaries would use the settlement option, so the first policies had not been based on mortality tables designed specifically for beneficiaries. However, by 1955, the settlement options had become very popular and placed a substantial long-term financial risk on the insurer after the death of the original insured. As a result, the industry needed a special table to value the long-range cost of such options.

The 1955 American Annuity Table was based on 1948-53 intercompany experience on settlement options. The rates were developed as a rough graduation of the underlying mortality experience. A separate female table was not developed, but in his paper, McCarter suggested that a five-year setback would be appropriate in determining rates for females. Experience below age 60 was extended as a ratio to the a-1949 Table. McCarter agreed that rates should be projected to the current year, but suggested use of a setback method rather than a projection scale. He recommended that the American Annuity Table be setback by 1/10th of a year of age for each year after 1955.

The next individual annuity table was the 1971 Individual Annuity Mortality Table.[23] The underlying table, based on 1960-67 intercompany experience, was called the 1963 Experience Table. The 1963 experience was projected to 1971 and rates were reduced 10% to provide a margin. In his paper, Cherry recommended that the table be used as a minimum standard without a projection, but if used for other purposes, the rates should be projected by Scale B.

The current table in this series is the 1983 Individual Annuity Mortality Table (1983 Table a). This table is based on 1971-76 annuity experience at ages 60 and higher. To provide a current mortality table, the experience was projected 9.5 years to 1983. The 1983 Basic Table was determined by application of actual-to-expected ratios to the 1971 IAM based on the projected 1971-76 experience. The final 1983 Table a was produced by first reducing the basic rates to build in a margin and by then graduating the results. (*TSA*, V.33, 675-750) Projection scale G was developed for use with this table.

Group Annuities

Most of the annuities in the United States are provided through pension plans covering groups of employees. As a result, there was an early interest in producing distinct group annuity mortality tables that would reflect the differences in mortality between group and individual annuities. In addition, these tables would have to reflect the differences in operation between the group and individual annuity markets. Individual annuities are typically purchased when the annuity payout is to begin, so that individual annuity experience is available, and individual annuity rates are required only from near retirement age (55 or 60) on. Group annuities are purchased as deferred annuities over the employee's working life and group annuity rates are required from the start of employment (age 15 or 20). However, until the employee actually retires, the financial incentive for group plans to maintain and provide accurate and detailed data is not great, and obtaining preretirement group annuity experience is difficult.

The first such table was the Combined Annuity Table created by blending Cammack's Clerical Mortality Table at the younger ages with the American Annuitant's Table at the older ages.[24] In his discussion of this table, Craig did not produce separate male and female tables but suggested that it was "very practical and advantageous...to assume that females would be rated down four years." (Craig, *Mortality*,p. 121)

Both the Combined and 1937 Standard Annuity Tables were used for group as well as individual business until the 1950s. Since 1951 there have been two separate families of annuity tables, with a new group table developed at the same time as each new individual table in both 1971 and 1983.

The 1949 Annuity Table for individual policies was closely followed by the Group Annuity Table for 1951 (Ga-1951) for group annuity mortality.[25] Ages over 65 were derived from group annuity experience from 1946 to 1950. The experience was projected three years by Jenkins and Lew's Scale B, and a 10% margin was built in by reducing the rates. The a-1949 Table was projected forward one year for the younger ages. With these adjustments, the final table was appropriate for 1951. In his paper, Peterson considered that neither Scales A nor B were appropriate for projection purposes for group annuities, so he introduced a Scale C with a higher rate of improvement.

The 1971 Individual Annuity Table had its counterpart in the 1971 Group Annuity Mortality (1971 GAM) Table. The 1971 GAM was projected from experience in 1964-68 and a margin of 8% to 10% was added.[26] Rates before age 60 were based on the Ga-1951 Table projected forward. The authors developed a Scale D for use in the projection to 1971 and added a Scale

E for males as more appropriate for the future than the earlier scales.

As with the 1971 IAM, the 1983 IAM had its counterpart in the 1983 Group Annuity Mortality Table.[27] The 1983 GAM differs from most other recent tables in that it is not based on a new study of experience. The committee which prepared the 1983 GAM projected the 1966 experience underlying the 1971 GAM to 1983 through the use of factors based largely on the United States population mortality experience. The rates were graduated and loaded to produce the 1983 GAM. The committee proposed a Scale H to be used for projections. This is a slight modification of the projection Scale G published for use with the 1983 Table a.[27]

Most of the larger pension plans are uninsured and have different characteristics and safety concerns than those of insured plans. The first in what may become a series of tables specifically designed for uninsured plans is the UP-1984 Table produced from experience of large uninsured pension plans. The U stands for Unisex since the table does not split male and female mortality and the P stands for Pension. The table was published in 1977, but projected to 1984.[28]

The UP-1984 Table was produced on a unisex basis in response to a Supreme Court decision that benefits paid from employer pension plans had to be the same for men and women. The decision did not prohibit use of sex-distinct tables for determining the liabilities of a pension plan, but many actuaries use the same unisex basis for the determination of optional benefits and the valuation of those benefits. Ironically, the move to unisex tables for annuities occurred at the same time as sex-distinct tables were first used in statutory individual insurance tables.

Projection methods have been used for annuities since 1949 with the Scales A and B presented by Jenkins and Lew. Although later scales from C to F had been suggested, Scale B remained the most popular through the early 1980s. The developers of the 1983 Table a suggested a projection scale G to be used in projecting the table past 1983. Scale B had assumed an annual improvement of 1.25% below age 50, but a reduction in the improvement to zero after age 90. Scale G assumes that the reduction for males will be higher at all ages with a maximum of 2% from 35 to 45, and that the improvement will decline to 1% a year after age 90. The Scale G reduction factor is around .25% per year higher for females.

The latest recommendation, included in the presentation of the 1983 GAM table, suggests use of a Scale H based on 1966 to 1983 trends. The Scale H improvement is around 2% a year at age 40; dropping gradually to .5% at age 92; with an ultimate rate of zero at age 100.

OTHER TABLES

Industrial Insurance

Another important family of mortality tables was developed for valuation of industrial insurance, which was once very popular in the United States and so named because the business was "conducted mainly among the industrial classes."[29] The premiums were paid in small weekly amounts collected at the insured's homes by the insurance agent. Industrial insurance policyholders were expected to have higher mortality than standard ordinary insurance policyholders for two reasons. First, medical selection was seldom used with industrial insurance policyholders and, second, the policies were written for people with lower income who would be expected to have higher mortality.

Before 1907, standard life insurance tables were used for industrial insurance. The first Standard Industrial Mortality Table was based on the experience of the Metropolitan Life Insurance Company between 1896 and 1905. The table was adopted as the standard for the state of New York in 1907.

At the request of the New York Insurance Department, in the 1930s the Metropolitan examined the experience of their business and found that, over all, industrial mortality was 128% of standard ordinary mortality. Therefore, the 1941 CSO then being developed would not have been adequate for industrial issues. This led to the 1941 Industrial Mortality Table, based on Metropolitan experience from 1930 to 1939.[30]

The 1961 Standard Industrial Table may be the last in the series of tables used for this vanishing breed of insurance. The table was developed from 1954 to 1958 intercompany experience.[31] The loading used for a safety margin for the 1961 industrial insurance was greater than in the 1958 CSO because it was expected that there would be a wider variation in experience among industrial than among individual companies.

Fraternal Organizations

The National Fraternal Congress held in 1897 recommended the development of a separate mortality table for Fraternal business. As with the American Experience Table, details on the construction were never published, but Elston assumed that the experience was largely from one large fraternal company - The Royal Arcanum. An interesting sidelight is reported by Elston. The table to be graduated was given to George D. Eldridge late in the afternoon of the day before the graduated table was due. Mr. Eldridge must have had a busy night because the next day he produced a completed Makehamized table that became the National Fraternal Congress Table of Mortality. (Elston, *Sources,* 71)

A second fraternal table, the Fraternal-American

Mortality Table, was produced in 1912. The table was developed by Fackler and Fackler by merging the first fraternal table at the younger ages with the American Experience Table at the older ages.[32]

COMPARISON OF TABLES

Charts II.3 and II.4 compare the remaining life expectancies at ages 20 and 60 for the various life and annuity tables to expectancies of the white male population from the 1900 through 1980 United States Life Tables. The life insurance tables are indicated by boxes and the annuity tables by triangles. Except for the American Experience Table, the life expectancies are shown in the year of publication. Thus, there are three CSO boxes -- for 1941, 1958 and 1980.

The life insurance tables show life expectancies very close to that of the general population. Actual life insurance experience is better than that of the general population, but this advantage is largely offset by the margins added to the mortality rates for safety.

Life expectancy from the annuitant tables is significantly higher than for the general population. Annuitants do tend to live longer than the general population, but this difference is increased by the margin built into annuity mortality rates.

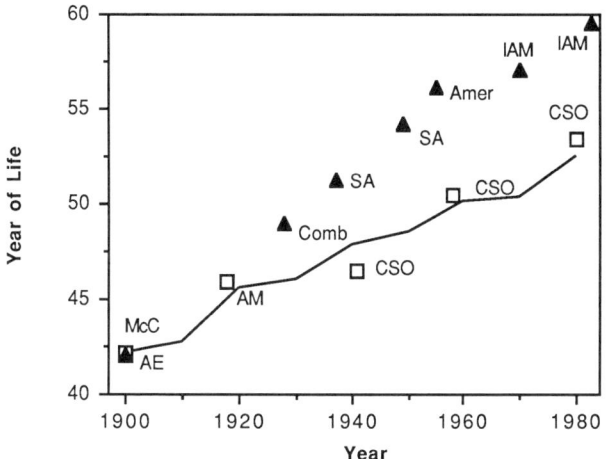

Chart II.3
Expectation of Life After 20 for Males

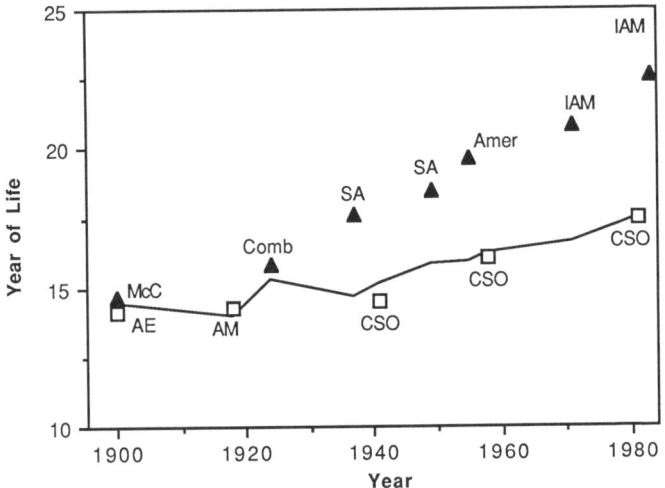

Chart II.4
Expectation of Life After 60 for Males

The next chapter will discuss the prospects for continuing improvement in the rates of mortality at various ages. As long as mortality improves, there will be a need for revised mortality tables for insurance and annuities.

The history of mortality tables suggests that there may be a set of new annuity mortality tables every decade. The experience will show that annuitants have better mortality than in the general population. The valuation table will show an even wider difference since the rates will be reduced to provide a safety margin.

History suggests that there will be a longer period between life insurance mortality tables since the natural reduction in mortality rates increases the safety margin in the tables. There will probably be a new table every generation. Life insurance mortality will usually be better than that of the general population. However, the increase in rates to provide a safety margin will bring the rates in the statutory table closer to the experience in the general population.

III. THE FUTURE OF MORTALITY

The United States population tables and other mortality studies show that there has been consistent improvement in mortality for at least the last 200 years. This chapter discusses the expectations for continued improvement in mortality concluding with a prediction of the shape and level of the mortality curve at the end of the second century of the actuarial profession in the United States.

The expectations for the level and shape of the mortality curve involve three separate but related questions. First, is there a law of mortality? A law of mortality would describe the underlying structure of any mortality table built from observations.

Second, is there a maximum life span? If there is an age at which almost all survivors would be expected to die then the table could confidently be ended at that point. This limiting age is not the same as the life expectancy. The life expectancy is approximately equal to the average age at death. The limiting age is the age at which the last survivor will die.

Third, what will be the rate of improvement in mortality at different ages? If this rate of improvement slows and eventually stops, the rate at that point will be the ultimate mortality rate.

GOMPERTZ AND OTHER LAWS OF MORTALITY

The scientific optimism of the nineteenth century, and progress toward discovery of underlying laws explaining observations in other fields, encouraged actuaries to believe that an underlying law of mortality could be discovered. Many actuaries believed that discovery of the underlying law only required gathering and analyzing more data and developing a valid theory to explain the data.

According to Jordan, the earliest proposed law was that of Abraham de Moivre in 1724.[33] DeMoivre's law was based on an assumption that the same number of people died at every age:

$$l_x = k(w-x)$$

where:

k = a constant number of deaths at each age,

w = the age at which the last person died, and

x = the current age, so

l_x = the number alive at the beginning of x.

DeMoivre's law was put forward as a method of simplifying annuity calculations and he noted that it was only a rough approximation of the actual pattern of mortality.

The most popular candidates for the law of mortality have been built on the theory that the *force of mortality* grows continuously from the youngest through the oldest ages. The force of mortality at age x is "a measure of the mortality *at the precise moment of attaining age x.*" [italics in original] (Jordan, *Life*, 13)

The first formula that closely matched a major part of the mortality curve was developed by Benjamin Gompertz in 1825. Gompertz "assumed that man's power to resist death decreases at a rate proportional to itself." (Jordan, *Life*, 21) This assumption led to the following formula:

$$u_x = Bc^x$$

where B and c are constants that vary with the table and,

u_x is the force of mortality at age x.

Gompertz suggested that two forces were involved in determining the law of mortality. The first, which is recognized in his formula, is that the force of mortality increases as age increases. The second, not recognized in his formula, is that there is a chance risk of death at any age.

Makeham carried Gompertz a step further by adding a constant factor (A) to the force of mortality for the chance risk of death at any age. This lead to the following general form for Makeham's law of mortality:

$$u_x = A + Bc^x$$

As the actuarial profession moved from the scientific optimism of the nineteenth century to the more practical outlook of the twentieth century, the hope for discovering a general formula of mortality largely disappeared. The current actuarial mathematics textbook notes that the search for, and use of, laws of mortality has "declined in recent years. Many feel that the belief in universal laws of mortality is naive."[34]

Makeham formulas have been shown to fit most tables in the age range of most interest to insurers. However, a Makeham table that fits for these ages will not be appropriate at the youngest and oldest ages. The mortality rates from a Makeham curve that fits well from age 30 to 90 will be close to the accidental rate at all ages below 20 and exceed 1.0 around age 100. However, mortality rates are higher than the accidental constant from birth to around age ten. And it is never certain that if there is a large group of people at a given advanced age that all will die in the next year. A complete law of mortality would have to allow for the three aspects of the mortality curve that are not found in Gompertz or Makeham.

There were two practical reasons to fit mortality tables to a Gompertz or Makeham formula even after most actuaries abandoned the search for an underlying law of mortality. First, if a mathematical formula could represent a body of data with little error, then it would be easy to graduate the table by defining the constants that best fit the curve to the underlying data. Second, if a table were fitted to the Gompertz or Makeham formula, joint and survivor functions could be developed from one mortality table. Both practical reasons have become much less important since high-speed computers can be used to quickly graduate raw data and generate survivor functions directly from mortality rates without approximations.

The search for a law is still of interest to some in the actuarial profession. David Brillinger's paper in 1961 discussed the common laws of mortality.[35] Brillinger observed that if "the human body is considered to be an element made up of many components whose lifetimes are independent and identically distributed then it follows that the force of mortality" can be expressed by a formula similar to that of Makeham or Gompertz. Brillinger developed a generalized law which incorporates both the Makeham and Gompertz laws as simplified versions.

W. H. Wetterstrand demonstrated that the Gompertz law was a good fit to modern mortality tables from age 30 to 90.[36] His 1981 paper illustrates the fit for life insurance mortality studies from 1947 through 1976. Wetterstrand also derived Gompertz parameters for thirty-three mortality tables and explained how the values of the constants could be used to summarize the relative patterns of the different tables. Of particular interest is that recent population, insurance and annuity tables all have a c value that implies force of mortality rates increasing at between 9% and 10.5%.

It now seems unlikely that actuaries will discover a complete law of mortality. However, Wetterstrand has shown that the Gompertz theory holds remarkably well for a long span of human life. He also showed that the value of c is within a close range in all of the tables.

Since the Gompertz curve fits well for a large part of the curve, and the mortality curve at older and younger ages is fairly predictable, a practical approach would be to base a mortality table on assumptions that quantify the following characteristics:

> The infant mortality rate, which is the rate of mortality in the first year of life.

> The accidental rate for children. This will be the lower limit of the mortality rates at the youngest ages.

> The age at which the mortality rate is the lowest.

> The age at which mortality from non-accidental causes begins to be significant. Mortality rates will increase geometrically at each age after this point.

The age at which the rate of increase begins to decelerate.

The ultimate rate of mortality and the age at which the rate is achieved.

IS THERE A MAXIMUM LIFE SPAN?

Many actuaries who have studied mortality believe that there is a fixed maximum span of life, or limiting age. According to this view, anyone reaching the limiting age will die very soon thereafter. If this view is correct, and if the mortality below that age continues to improve, the survivor curve will be "squared." As mortality improves at all but the limiting age, there will eventually be very few deaths until the limiting age. The number of survivors at each age will approach a straight line close to the number of births and drop sharply near the limiting age. In other words, the mortality rate will be close to zero until the limiting age when it will jump to a value of 1.0.

Actuaries and other professionals interested in this question attended a symposium on *The Future of Life Expectancy* in Chicago in 1980.[37] Theodore J. Gordon lead off the symposium by suggesting, in the first chapter of the proceedings of the symposium, that while there had been significant improvement in mortality at most ages there was a limiting age of approximately 110 years. Gordon stated that there had been almost no change in this limiting age over the last 100,000 years and a survey completed by the participants indicated agreement with this point. Three-fourths of the participants assigned a low probability to an extension of the limiting age to 125 by the year 2020 and very few expected an extension to 150 years. However, there was no evidence presented in the proceedings either supporting a limiting age or showing why that age was around 110.

Shigekazu Hishinuma conducted an extensive survey of mortality experience for a paper presented to the Institute of Actuaries of Japan.[38] In his study of mortality experience from many sources and societies extending back to the Bronze Age, Hishinuma observed that there appeared to be a limiting age and suggested it might be around 120 to 130 years.

The early developers of mortality tables assigned a limiting age to their tables for practical as much as for theoretical reasons. Actuaries compute insurance and annuity functions working backward from the oldest age. Therefore it was essential to establish an age at which the last person would be expected to die and the younger the limiting age, the shorter the computations.

Homans had adopted age 96 as the limiting age for the American Experience table because at that time there was no record of an insured individual reaching age 100 in Europe or the United States. He described the use of 96 as the limiting age as "more of a happy accident, or a happy thought, than anything else." (Homans, *Response*,33) The 1941 CSO moved to age 99 as the limiting age, and this limiting age was also used in the later CSO Tables. Life insurance premiums and reserves are not greatly affected by mortality at the oldest ages, so use of the traditional limiting age of 99 does not present any problems, even though many insured people today live well past age 99.

In contrast, the limiting of annuity tables has received almost continual attention. As early as 1899, McClintock's Table moved the limiting age to 105. The 1937 Standard Annuity Table moved to a limiting age of 109; the 1955 American Annuity Table moved to 114; and the 1971 IAM moved to 115. The use of age 115 for the 1971 IAM was selected because age 115 was the first point at which a Makeham projection of the age 60 to 99 rates exceeded .95. The 1983 IAM continued to use 115 but the 1983 GAM used the same 110 limiting age as the 1971 GAM.

The reason for this attention is the periodic nature of annuity payments, and it is important that an annuity mortality table not underestimate potential payments at each and every age. An important component of this is the selection of a limiting age for the table that is just higher than the age at which the last payments might reasonably be expected. The financial effect of the limiting age is quite insignificant at the age at which payments begin under the typical annuity contract, but becomes progressively more important as the age of the annuitant advances.

The current actuarial textbook supports the limiting age concept and concludes that "For human lives there have been few observations of age-at-death beyond 110. Consequently, it is often assumed that there is an age...called the *limiting age.*" [italics in original] (Bowers, *Actuarial*, 53)

The weight of actuarial opinion and tradition supports a limiting age. However, recent actuarial studies support a maximum mortality rate of less than 50% with no limiting age.

The studies that traced individuals in a closed group until the last person died, mentioned in Chapter I, suggest a maximum rate of between 30% and 50%. A detailed study of data from the National Center for Health Statistics[39] by John Wilkin supported a mortality curve that levelled off at around 33% as the century point approached. Wilkin's study, and another study by Esther Portnoy,[40] also note that the mortality difference between males and females may disappear, and even cross over, at the oldest ages. Portnoy suggested methods to determine if an observed crossover is significant.

These studies support mortality rates that rise to a high level at around age 100 with little or no growth thereafter. While there is no limiting age as such, an annual mortality rate of 50% results in a low expectation that anyone will live as long as twenty years after the maximum mortality rate is reached. If, for instance, 10,000 people reach age 100 in a year, and the mortality rate is 50% a year after age 100, the last survivor would be expected to die by age 115. This explains why, even if there is no theoretical limiting age, there have been few, if any, legitimate reports of people who live beyond age 115 even in the largest healthiest populations. However, in the future, the mortality improvements at younger ages and the increase in the United States population in the twentieth century should greatly increase the number surviving past 100 in the twenty-first century. If there is no limiting age, then there should be many people surviving to age 120 and older in the next century.

The Gompertz and Makeham laws do not necessarily predict a limiting age. In fact, the annual rate of death approaches but never exceeds unity. However, a Gompertz or Makeham curve that fits well below age 90 will approach an annual mortality rate of 1.0 shortly after age 100. Bayo and Faber suggested that the Gompertz formula might fit well at the older ages if the value of c were lowered after age 85. (*TSA XXXV*,58)

Chart III.1 compares the actual observations with the limiting ages used in actuarial tables and predictions of the ultimate limiting age.

Chart III.1

The Limiting Age of Mortality

Observed	Age	Mortality Table	Predicted
	90		
		Amer Exp (1868)	
		1980 CSO	
	100		
		McClintock (1899)	
Bayo (1985)			
			Symposium (1980)
	110		
Lew (1986)			
		1983 IAM	
	120		Hishinuma (1976)

IMPROVEMENTS IN MORTALTY

The steady improvement in mortality throughout the twentieth century continues a trend that began in the eighteenth century. Hishinuma concluded that there had been little improvement in life expectancy until the advances in health care and hygiene beginning in the eighteenth century. Life expectancy at birth had ranged between 25 and 30 years from the Bronze age (3500 to 1400 B.C.) to the eighteenth century. By the middle of the nineteenth century, life expectancy at birth had increased to 35 years and by 1900 life expectancy had improved to 45 years. Today life expectancy averages around 75 years.

In summary, in the 5,000 years before the eighteenth century, there was little or no improvement in mortality. Life expectancy at birth increased by about five years from the middle of the eighteenth to the middle of the nineteenth century, ten more years by the end of the nineteenth century, and 30 more years in the first 80 years of the twentieth century.

Actuaries have made varying predictions about how much more improvement there may be in the mortality curve. Before 1949, mortality tables were not accompanied by suggested projection methods and factors. The authors of some of the tables noted that mortality appeared to be improving, but they did not have the information needed to measure the improvement. McClintock had observed that great progress in medicine and hygiene suggested that mortality in the twentieth century would be substantially improved over that of the nineteenth century. However, he thought that "adopting a basis of valuation which we know to be abundantly safe" (McClintock, *Special*, 14) would provide adequate safety. Even as late as 1918, the evidence for improvement was often masked by traumatic events.

Hishinuma noted that the highest expectation of life in the early 1970s was in Sweden with values of 72 years for males and 78 years for females. Based on a projection of improvements in mortality from different categories of disease, he estimated that the longest life expectancy would be 77.4 years for males and 81.7 years for females. He assumed that there would be an end to significant improvements in mortality by the time these expectancies were reached.

Wade observed that the life expectancy in the United States was 71.5 years for males and 78.5 years for females in 1987. She also examined improvement in mortality from categories of diseases to predict a life expectancy under the Social Security actuaries' projection *iii* assumptions of 83.6 years for males and 90.1 years for females in the year 2080. The Social Security actuaries' projection *ii* assumptions predict a life span of 78.2 years for males and 84.9 for females in 2080. The projection *iii* assumptions are also known as the "pessimistic assumptions" because greater improvements in mortality result in higher Social Security payouts. (Wade, *Social*,13)

The participants in the 1980 symposium on the *Future of Life Expectancy* predicted that the life expectancy for the population would increase to between 77 and 82 years of age by the year 2020.

There are possible events that could slow or reverse the improvement in mortality. The AIDS epidemic, resulting from the human immunodeficiency virus, could eventually wipe out or dampen mortality gains. Alternatively, a nuclear war could set the mortality curve back to where it was 200 years ago. However, it is more likely that the mortality rates at the end of the twenty-first century will be much lower than they are today.

MORTALITY IN THE TWENTY-FIRST CENTURY

While it appears unlikely that a complete law of mortality will ever be discovered, the Gompertz Law has been shown to hold very well for a long span of the mortality table. A geometric rate of increase takes over almost all mortality tables by the mid-forties. With the geometric growth as a core, the rest of the table can be constructed by extending the mortality to the very young and very old ages from observed patterns. This section presents alternative tables based on the observed patterns and compares these to other projections and the 1980 United States Life Tables.

The 1987 Public Health Service study shows that

the United States infant mortality rate (the rate in the first year of life) had decreased from 13.1 per 1,000 to 10.8 per 1,000 in the five years between 1979 and 1984. Comparison to other countries suggests that substantial additional improvement is possible. The lowest rate studied by the PHS, 6.0 per 1,000, occurred in Japan. If the trend continues, it is possible that the infant mortality rate can drop to 1 in 1,000 by the end of the twenty-first century.

The mortality rate in the early teens is usually the lowest rate. In the 1980 United States Life Tables, this rate had dropped below 2 in 10,000, half the rate in the 1960 tables. Further improvements might reduce the pure accidental rate to 1 in 10,000. Mortality in the first year of life is substantially higher, but the rate drops quickly and remains close to the lowest point through the mid-teens.

In the late teens and early twenties, the accidental death rate increases significantly, largely as a result of deaths from automobile accidents among young men eligible for driver's licenses. There is also a significant number of suicides at these ages. As a result, the non-health related death rate in the mid-twenties is three to five times higher than the lowest rate.

The ultimate trend at the oldest ages has not yet been demonstrated because of a paucity of observations. Many actuaries believe that the rate will increase geometrically at the oldest ages and eventually approach 1.0 at the limiting age at which almost all survivors die. Others believe that the mortality rate levels off somewhere between 300 and 500 deaths out of 1,000 alive at the oldest ages. Another possibility, in line with the "squaring" of the survivor curve, is for continual improvement at almost all advanced ages, but with a relatively inviolate limiting age of life.

These observations suggest a number of characteristics of the mortality table in the year 2089 (a hundred years from now). These characteristics, as compared to the 1980 United States Life Tables, are given in Chart III.2.

Charts III.3 and III.4 show two possibilities for the rates of mortality that might be observed in 100 years based on the characteristics in Chart III.2. Table A is constructed with a limiting age of 130. Table B has no limiting age, but approaches a maximum rate of 400 per 1,000. The two tables are the same through age 87. After that point the B rates are less than the A rates. For these purposes Tables A and B may be regarded as the limits of population or unisex mortality. These Tables are compared to the male and female mortality in the 1980 United States Life Tables.

Chart III.2

Characteristics of Oberved and Expected Mortality Tables

1980 United States Life Tables

Characteristic	Males	Females	Expected 2089
Infant mortality rate	12/1,000	10/1,000	1/1,000
Lowest rate	.2/1,000	.2/1,000	.1/1,000
at age	11	11	11
Age at which geometric increase begins	35	29	35
Age at which increase decelerates	85	95	100
Maximum rate	395/1,000	370/1,000	400/1,000
Reached at	109	109	113

Chart III.3

Current and Projected Mortality Rates

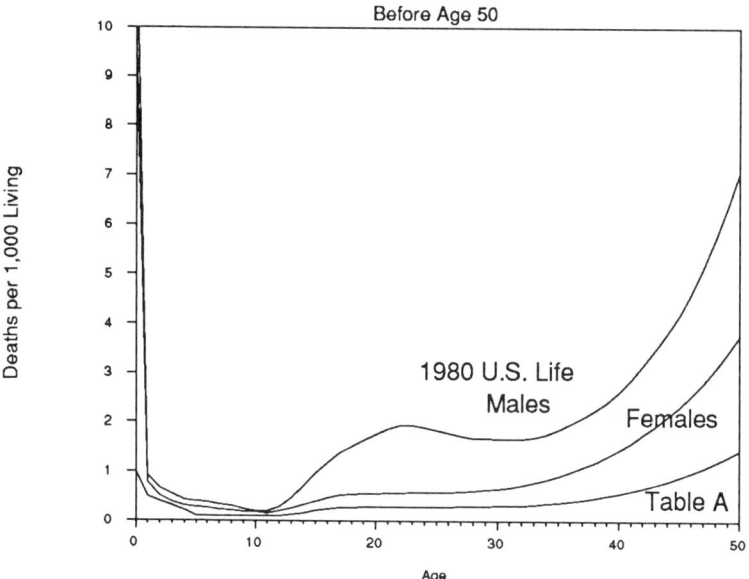

Chart III.4

Current and Projected Mortality Rates

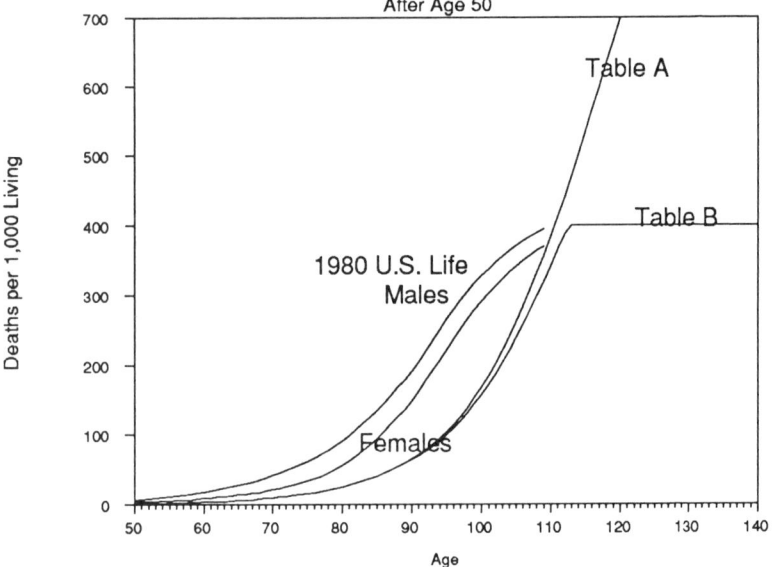

Tables A and B have life expectancies that are close to those predicted by the projection *iii* assumptions of the Social Security actuaries and by Scale H applied to the 1983 GAM. However, the tables project life expectancies that are much higher than those suggested by Hishinuma and the symposium participants. This paper ends with a comparison of those predictions in Chart III.5. Since very few people live to the point at which the rates in tables A and B diverge, the average life expectancy is almost the same for both tables. The demonstration that will confirm one of the predictions, or, more likely, deny them all, can only be made by actuaries as yet unborn.

Chart III.5

Predicted Expectations of Life at Birth

	Male	Unisex	Female
1980 United States Life Tables	70.8 yrs.		77.6 yrs.
Predicted by			
Hishimuma	77.4		81.7
Symposium for 2020		82	
1983 GAM with Scale H		88.3	
Social Security			
i	75.2		81.5
ii	78.2		84.9
iii	83.6		90.1
Table A		87.8	
Table B		87.9	

NOTES

CHAPTER I

MORTALITY IN THE UNITED STATES

1. Robert J. Myers and Franciso R. Bayo, "United States Life Tables for 1979-81," *Transactions of the Society of Actuaries* 37(1985): 303-350.

2. National Center for Health Statistics, *Health, United States, 1987*, DHHS Pub. No. (PHS)88-1232. Public Health Service (Washington, D.C.: U.S. Government Printing Office, Mar. 1988): 10-11.

3. Alice H. Wade, *Social Security Area Population Projections: 1988*, Actuarial Study No. 102.(Baltimore, Md.: The U.S. Dept. of Health and Human Services).

4. Francisco R. Bayo and Joseph F. Faber, "Mortality Experience around Age 100," *Transactions of the Society of Actuaries* 35(1983): 37-64.

5. Edward A. Lew and Laurence Garfinkel, "Mortality at Ages 65 and Over in a Middle-Class Population, *Transactions of the Society of Actuaries* 36(1984): 257-308.

CHAPTER II

MORTALITY TABLES USED BY ACTUARIES IN THE UNITED STATES

6. Tillinghast/Towers Perrin, *Principal Mortality Tables OLD and NEW*(Atlanta:T/TP, 1987).

7. "Report of the Special Committee to Recommend New Mortality Tables for Valuation of Individual Ordinary Insurance," *Transactions of the Society of Actuaries 33*(1981): 621.

8. "Report of the Committee to Recommend a New Mortality Basis for Individual Annuity Valuation (Derivation of the 1983 Table a)," *Transactions of the Society of Actuaries 33*(1981): 675-750.

9. James S. Elston, *Sources and Characteristics of the Principal Mortality Tables* (2d ed.)(New York: Actuarial Society of America, 1932).

10. Sheppard Homans, "Response to Toasts," *Transactions Actuarial Society of America I*(1889-1890): 33.

11. Arthur Hunter, "Should the 'American Men' Mortality Table (A.M.) be the Basis for Premiums and Reserves?," *Transactions Actuarial Society of America 20*(1919): 23-40.

12. John S. Thompson, "The Commissioners 1941 Standard Ordinary Mortality Table," *Transactions Actuarial Society of America* 42(1941): 314.

13. Charles M. Sternhill, "The New Standard Ordinary Mortality Table," *Transactions of the Society of Actuaries* 9(1957): 1-23.

"General," *Transactions of the Society of Actuaries* 10(1958): 686-715.

14. Society of Actuaries, Committee on Ordinary Insurance and Annuities, "1965-70 Basic Tables," *Transactions of the Society of Actuaries 1973 Reports of Mortality and Morbidity*: 199-224.

Society of Actuaries Committee on Ordinary Insurance and Annuities, "1975-80 Basic Tables," *Transactions of the Society of Actuaries 1982 Reports of Mortality and Morbidity Experience*: 55-82.

15. Morton D. Miller, "The Commissioners 1960 Standard Group Mortality Table and 1961 Standard Group Life Insurance Premium Rates," *Transactions of the Society of Actuaries* 13(1961): 586.

16. E. E. Cammack, "Mortality Tables Constructed Upon the Experience under Group Policies," *Transactions Actuarial Society of America* 28(1927): 247-261.

17. Michael Demner, "Group Life Insurance Mortality," Part 5 Study Notes,(Chicago: Society of Actuaries, 1977).

18. Emory McClintock, "Special Tables for the Estimation of Mortality Among Annuitants," *Transactions Actuarial Society of America 6* (1899-1900): 13.

19. Arthur Hunter, "Mortality among American Annuitants and Premiums Based Thereon," *Transactions Actuarial Society of America 21*(1920): 157-177.

20. Frank D. Kineke, "A New Annuity Mortality Table," *Transactions Actuarial Society of America 39*(1938): 8-23.

21. Wilmer A. Jenkins and Edward A. Lew, "A New Mortality Basis for Annuities," *Transactions of the Society of Actuaries 1*(1949): 369-466.

22. William C. McCarter, "A New Annuity Mortality Table and A Graded Rate System for the Life Insurance Settlement Options," *Transactions of the Society of Actuaries 8*(1956): 127-165.

23. Harold Cherry, "The 1971 Individual Annuity Mortality Table," *Transactions of the Society of Actuaries 23*(1971): 475-550.

24. J. D. Craig, discussion of "Mortality Table Constructed Upon the Experience under Group Policies," published in *Transactions Actuarial Society of America* 29(1928): 118-127.

Robert Henderson, "Joint Life Annuity Values by the Combined Annuity Mortality Table," *Transactions Actuarial Society of America* 31(1930): 62-71.

25. Ray M. Peterson, "Group Annuity Mortality," *Transactions of the Society of Actuaries* 4(1952): 246-307.

26. Harold R. Greenlee, Jr. and Alfonso Keh, "The 1971 Group annuity Mortality Table," *Transactions of the Society of Actuaries 23(1971): 569-664.*

27. Committee on Annuities, "Development of the 1983 Group Annuity Mortality Table," *Transactions of the Society of Actuaries* 35(1983): 859-899.

28. William W. Fellers and Paul H. Jackson, "Noninsured Pensioner Mortality The UP-1984 Table," *The Proceedings Conference of Actuaries in Public Practice* 25(1975-1976):456-502.

29. J. D. Buchanan, "Industrial Life Insurance," *Transactions of the Actuarial Society of America 22* (1921): 36.

30. Actuarial Society of America and American Institute of Actuaries, *Actuarial Tables: 1941 Standard Industrial Mortality Tables. 2 1/2%.* ASA and AIA, 1946.

31. William C. Brown, "A Proposed New Industrial Valuation Table," *Transactions of the Society of Actuaries* 13(1961): 457-494.

32. Edward B. Fackler, "The Fraternal-American Mortality Table," *Proceedings of the Fraternal Actuarial Association* 8(1925-1926): 17-26.

CHAPTER III

THE FUTURE OF MORTALITY

33. Chester Wallace Jordan, *Life Contingencies*, 2d ed.(Chicago: Society of Actuaries, 1967).

34. Newton L. Bowers, Jr., Hans U. Gerber, James C. Hickman, Donald A. Jones, and Cecil J. Nesbitt, *Actuarial Mathematics*.(Itasca, Ill: Society of Actuaries, 1986): 71.

35. David R. Brillinger, "A Justification of Some Common Laws of Mortality," *Transactions of the Society of Actuaries 13*(1961): 118.

36. W. H. Wettershand, "Parametric Models for Mortality Data: Gompertz's Law over Time," *Transactions of the Society of Acturies 33*(1981): 159-176.

37. Society of Actuaries, Association of Life Insurance Medical Directors of America, and Home Office Life Underwriters Association, *The Future of Life Expectancy; Economic, Social and Medical Implicatons of Living Longer*, Proceedings of a symposium held March 10-11, 1980 in Chicago, Ill.,(Chicago, Ill.: SOA, ALIMDA, and HOLUA).

38. Shigekazu Hishinuma, "Historical Review on the Longevity of the Human Beings." Society of Actuaries Library, Schaumburg, Ill.

39. John C. Wilkin, "Recent Trends in the Mortality of the Aged," *Transactions of the Society of Actuaries* 33(1981): 11-44.

40. Esther Portnoy, "Crossover in Mortality Rates by Sex," *Transactions of the Society of Actuaries* 38(1986): 229-241.

INDEX TO MORTALITY AND RELATED TABLES

Numeric values for these tables are not given in this publication. The Tillinghast publication is one source for many of these values.

a-1949
  See 1949 Standard Annuity

Actuaries
  See Combined Experience

American Annuitants (1920), 42, 46

1955 American Annuity, 44, 65

American Experience (1868), 31-33, 34, 52, 64

American Men Ultimate (1918, $Am^{(5)}$), 34, 40

1960 Basic Group
  See 1960 Commissioners Standard Group

1941 Basic Table
  See 1941 Commissioners Standard Ordinary

1958 Basic Table
  See 1958 Commissioners Standard Ordinary

1965-70 Basic Tables, 38

1975-80 Basic Tables, 38

1980 Basic Table
  See 1983 Commissioners Standard Ordinary

1983 Basic Table
See 1983 Individual Annuity

Cammack (1927), 24, 33, 40

Cammack Clerical (1927), 40, 46

Carlisle (1815), 30-31

Cause of Death, 7-10

Combined Annuity (1928), 46, 47

Combined Experience (1843), 30-31

1958 Commissioners Extended Term (1958 CET)
See 1958 Commissioners Standard Ordinary

1980 Commissioners Extended Term (1980 CET)
See 1980 Commissioners Standard Ordinary

1960 Commissioners Standard Group (1960 CSG), 24, 40, 41

1941 Commissioners Standard Ordinary (1941 CSO), 32, 35, 36, 40, 65

1958 Commissioners Standard Ordinary (1958 CSO), 35-37, 41

1980 Commissioners Standard Ordinary (1980 CSO), 23, 24, 28, 29, 33, 36-38

1963 Experience
See 1971 Individual Annuity

Fraternal-American (1912), 51-52

Ga-51
  See 1951 Group Annuity

1951 Group Annuity (1951 GAM), 24, 47

1971 Group Annuity (1971 GAM), 47, 65

1983 Group Annuity (1983 GAM), 26, 28, 48, 65

Health Male (1862, H^m), 30-31

1971 Individual Annuity (1971 IAM), 45, 47, 65

1983 Individual Annuity (1983 IAM), 24, 28, 45, 65, 77

McClintock (1899), 24, 29, 41, 65

National Fraternal Congress (1898), 51

Northamption (1783), 30

Projection Scale B, 43, 45, 47, 49

Projection Scale C, 47

Projection Scale G, 45, 49

Projection Scale H, 48, 49, 77

Projection Scales (General), 28, 43, 47-48, 49, 69

1937 Standard Annuity (1937 SA), 42-43, 47, 65

1949 Standard Annuity (1949 SA), 43, 44

Standard Industrial (1906), 24, 50

1941 Standard Industrial (1941 SI), 50-51

1961 Standard Industrial (1961 SI), 51

1983 Table a
See 1983 Individual Annuity

1983 Table A
See 1983 Individual Annuity

1984 Unisex Pension
See UP-84

1949-51 United States Life Table, 35

1979-81 United States Life Table, 1, 10, 12-17, 19, 71-76

United States Life Tables (general), 1-7, 10-11, 19- 22, 52-54

UP-84, 26, 48-49